POETRY NOW YEARBOOK 2003

Edited by

Heather Killingray

First published in Great Britain in 2003 by
POETRY NOW
Remus House,
Coltsfoot Drive,
Peterborough, PE2 9JX
Telephone (01733) 898101
Fax (01733) 313524

SB ISBN 1 84460 760 7

Foreword

Although we are a nation of poets we are accused of not reading poetry, or buying poetry books. After many years of listening to the incessant gripes of poetry publishers, I can only assume that the books they publish, in general, are books that most people do not want to read.

Poetry should not be obscure, introverted, and as cryptic as a crossword puzzle: it is the poet's duty to reach out and embrace the world.

The world owes the poet nothing and we should not be expected to dig and delve into a rambling discourse searching for some inner meaning.

The reason we write poetry (and almost all of us do) is because we want to communicate: an ideal; an idea; or a specific feeling. Poetry is as essential in communication, as a letter; a radio; a telephone, and the main criterion for selecting the poems in this anthology is very simple: they communicate.

CONTENTS

The Master Of The Sonnet

Oh bard, who lauded nature's wealth
with which moral moles surrounded,
concisely did you cite ill-health
society deemed unfounded.

'This world', Wordsworth, charges me still
to value that which most may pass -
to seek the song sung by each rill,
the sculpture fluffed by each cloud-mass.

But shadows impotent these words -
poor dim reflections of your skill
which failed, in turn, to capture birds,
forests, seas, dales and daffodils.

Dare none your soaring fame impede,
whom tilled rich soil with searching seed.

Perry McDaid

PANDORA'S BOX

We never touched
Pandora's Box
- we left it closed,
each time we glanced
at sunlight dancing
on the locks

. . . and if we'd opened it,
by now
we'd hurt each other
having rows,
I wouldn't flirt
with you . . . by now

We never took it
all the way,
but that's now
for the best
I'd say -

we never told
each other lies
and love still burns
within your eyes

so let's postpone
the final act
and leave Pandora's
box intact.

Jennifer D Wootton

THE WOODPIGEON

The evening's tranquillity
ended abruptly
as the cat came into view.
Everyone shouted and clapped,
Alison threw her fork
and at last, the cat was chased off.

Next began the pantomime dash
around the garden, as the pigeon
flutter-hopped across the lawn,
eventually seeking sanctuary
beneath the rose bushes.

I laughed, darted, lunged
at the frightened bird,
as somehow it always
stayed one jump ahead.
When caring hands finally closed
around delicate breast
and felt sticky wetness
I stopped laughing.

The audience went quiet too,
and took a step back; left me
centre stage, holding the pigeon.
Useless hands quickly turned crimson
as the bird's tiny heart
hammered against my palm,
faltered, and then ceased.

Bonita Hall

In The Realms Of Dead Poets

I dwell, in the realms of dead poets
Lost, in the haunts of distant dreams
Void of pain, in a world of transcendent spirits
Forgotten souls whose work will exist for aeons
I weep for their beauty; beauty which must die
Ephemeral years of glory in fading health
Sharing implicit thoughts of hope, fear and vulnerability
Opening windows into their souls; a stark vision of oneself
Shrouding themselves in twilight scenes of imagery
Unknown lives yet posthumously receiving immortal fame
Existing merely in terms of poetic soliloquy
Few are remembered but none died in vain
Creating vistas of pure, undefiled freedom
And I bask in their enigmatic visions of Elysium.

Steven J Smith

Dr Stella

No sense in wasting time
On old flames
Head's still on running
In this the first time

Great lady great feet
Means to an end
Your place in society
What else other than Dr Stella

All over the world
Everyone on the chatter line
Talking it over this situation
Congratulations to Dr Stella.

S M Thompson

WORKOUT

Battling the bulge in a quest to be slim
The vitamin junkies flock to the gym
Anabolic steroids and testosterone flying
As would be Rambos pump some iron
Wall to wall mirrors to scrutinise
Every lump and dimple of those cellulite thighs
Pounding the treadmill, watching the reflection
Working up a sweat, in search of perfection
Adrenaline surging through every vein
Grimacing the motto 'No pain, no gain'
Bodies squeezed into figure-hugging lycra
With a burning desire to be a few pounds lighter.

Sharon Brewer

Clowning

A man with bright
Orange hair and . . .
A devil may care
Attitude is most
Significant meanings are in
Abundance is there for
Everyone has something to
Offer up your dreams
Tonight is under a full
Moon at me I'll dance for
You get what you
Give me time, I'll show you
Love is all you
Need and greed squeeze dry
Life is not to be taken too
Seriously though I must go
Now is all I have.

Clare West

GOLDEN WEDDING

We've been together fifty years,
And never a single row,
I didn't believe that story then,
And I don't believe it now.

If two people live together,
And always think alike,
Think how boring it would be,
Each day and every night,

You need to have a challenge,
Each other's views to compare,
And give and take a little,
To show you really care,

I suppose that I've been lucky,
And I hope that he has too,
In finding someone who really cares,
And wants the best for you.

I Covell

The Sick In Mind Society

4.30 in the morning loud rapping on the wall,
next door neighbour rousing us, a very urgent call.
Inferno in the car park someone has set our car on fire,
we dash out feeling helpless still in our night attire.

The car's a complete write off, went up like a torch.
Firemen sympathetic as they make out their report.
Now we senior citizens are left bemused and sad
that someone so vindictive has treated us so bad.

It is not just financial loss we find so hard to bear
but dreadful inconvenience as the car was always there.
Now we cannot reach the shops, our holidays are ruined
because we cannot walk far we must try to use the buses

Which do not often run on time, they are infrequent too,
which makes our lives so hard at seventy six and eighty two.
I wish that I could understand why people act the way they do.
Is something lacking in their lives? The many suffering for the few.

Who is to blame I wonder for our sick world today.
I do not know the answer but the price we all must pay.

Ruth Barclay Brook

Passion

I look at you in greedy anticipation.

Already my hands are busy,
unable to resist the urge
to rip away whatever covers you
and caress your smoothness.

My tongue touches you,
delicately,
letting your taste linger,

anticipating the moment of consummation,
the rush of adrenalin
the unleashing of endorphins
the melting of you into me.

Oh, how I love chocolate.

Marion Porter

In Car Rules

Here are some rules whilst in your car.
Do not ignore or you'll not get far.
Do not develop a very bad habit -
Silence rules - you must not rabbit.
Keep both hands upon your wheel;
Keep your elbow off the sill.

Do not speed of pick your nose;
Wind down windows, adjust your clothes;
No snogging, drinking, smokes nor eat;
No looking down towards your feet.
Be caught on film in a speed trap -
What's that hand doing in your lap?

Sedate your children, pets and wives,
So you won't injure other's lives.
Mobile phones should be turned off.
You must not laugh, or sneeze, or cough.
Make up your face or squeeze that pimple.
Rules in the car are not too simple.

To drive without due care/attention
Leads to a fine and prosecution.
A boost in sales throughout the land
Someone's produced a prosthetic hand.
Place this firmly to grip your wheel,
It fools the camera and The Bill!

B P Paxman

BORDERLINER

Over the borderline
Over the edge
Is it far to fall?
No, like riding a bike
With a wobbly wheel
Or balancing on a ball.

As thin as a Rizla
For rolling a smoke
Blown away in the breeze,
Or the cutting edge
Of a razor blade
Easy as shelling peas.

Was it soft where you fell?
Did it hurt you like hell
As you shook the dust from your hair?
As your ego got dented
Your anger was vented -
'There's no one to kiss me well'.

Did you rush for a drink
To lessen the pain
Medicine to make you feel fine?
As it slid down your throat
And oozed through your veins
'Hey, give me just one more red wine.'

The relapse is here
The damage is done
What the heck you've been here before
Just go with the flow
Hang on with both hands
To the glass that promises you more.

Hang on to that dream
Hang on to your life
Or is something taking you over?
Is it you? Is it them?
Is it out there or in here?
'Hell, I'd better have another'.

The long journey home
Feels like treading in mud
Bouncing from wall to wall,
Tomorrow will come
Sure as eggs are eggs,
Can you ever get back on that ball?

Sylvia Ross

SOPHIE

I've a memory of Sophie
Who's a girl I never knew
One who left a tiny message
Back in 1852
And although she's long since left the world
Her message travelled far
Scratched deep into the castle wall
'Sophie and Papa'.

Who were you little Sophie
When among these stones you passed?
And did you think your message
Like the ones before would last?
That however old this monument
The silence of its stones
Would be drowned by all the signatures
Etched out as time has flown?

Did you pass by 'CW'
From 1704?
Whose neatly carved initials
Hide beside a ghostly door
Or were you in the dungeon?
Did you see around the walls
The shaken names of prisoners
Their souls about to fall?

And did you ever stop to think
Along with your papa
That one day some strange passer by
Would wonder who you are?
Perhaps you did - I'll never know
But while I think of you
I'll leave my name alongside yours
From 1852.

Mark Gilronan

People's Pedlary

(After Dream-Pedlary by Thomas Lovell Bedoes 1803-1849)

If there were dreams to sell
What would you buy?
Visions that drugs foretell,
Faiths that your gods deny,
Gleanings the reapers leave;
Fables the spin-men weave.

If there were lies to sell
What would you buy?
Killers with tales to tell,
Virtues, which lusts defy,
Branding each hawk a dove;
Swearing to die for love.

If there was love to sell
What would you buy?
Stories of kiss and tell,
Headlines to catch the eye;
Honour too cheaply sold;
Secrets for Judas-gold.

If there were truths to sell
What would you buy?
Spielers to cast a spell,
Sermons to craft a lie;
Tricksters of pedlar's art.
Hawkers, who play their part:

If there was truth to tell.

Alan Chesterfield

AERIAL THRILLS AT KILL DEVIL HILLS, DEC 17TH 1903

At North Carolina's Kill Devil Hills
On a crisp December day,
An event of exhilaration
Blew gravity's limits away.
Flyer 1 took off triumphantly,
And Orville and Wilbur Wright
Achieved their great ambition
Of sustained, controllable flight.

Consider again the importance
Of this epochal attempt,
When a powered machine of motion
Fulfilled all they must have dreamt
Of, an incredible accomplishment
That amazed the eager world
To what could now be possible
With the open sky unfurled.

David Coates

How Time Flies

A year has passed since I took my retirement,
A time I anticipated with much enjoyment!
Acquaintances asked, 'What will you do?
There will only be boredom ahead of you.'
Colleagues said, 'Oh I wish it were me!
How I'd love it at last to be really free.'
Others said, 'You'll never ever fill your time.'
But I was fairly sure all would be fine.
I've visited family living very far away,
To go to Australia really made my day.
My daughter has moved, lots of work there,
And I help all I can because I care.
I've helped to redecorate our home too,
For prior to this year I had too much else to do.
My dogs have enjoyed my company more,
Walking after a full day's work could be a chore.
I've had more time to sit and read,
A pastime I enjoy very much indeed.
I've given the garden much more care,
Lots of lovely plants are growing there.
My husband asks, 'How did you manage before?'
I reply, 'Because I had to be organised more.'
I go to line dancing classes and keep fit
I've even lost weight I must admit!
I still have lots more things to try
But my oh my, how time does fly!

Christine Naylor

I Want To Be An Elf

I want to be an elf.
I want to roam Middle Earth.
Help me be an elf.

Serene and master of myself.
One of noble birth.
I want to be an elf.

For the sake of my health,
Fitness and a reduction in girth,
Help me be an elf.

With sublime music in wealth,
Graceful and full of mirth,
I want to be an elf.

My sword sworn to protect yourself;
Mistress Galadriel: your serf!
Help me be an elf.

There's no magic ring in the books on my shelf.
Of any adventure, in my life, there's a dearth.
I want to be an elf.
Help me be an elf.

Allyson Cole

CARE IN THE COMMUNITY

I have no home, where shall I go?
I shake my head 'cause I don't know,
My clothes are dirty I can tell,
Though they tell me that my mind's unwell.

Flashbacks of my mother's touch,
A nice warm house I loved so much,
But that I think was long ago,
I shake my head 'cause I don't know.

The sky gets dark and now I'm cold,
I wonder why I look so old?
I can't remember when I ate,
The voices in my head debate.

It's bedtime and I fear once more,
To close my eyes by some shop door,
I gently rock myself to sleep,
And pray to God my soul to keep.

E A S

Night Call

A flicker of candlelight
Illuminates the wall
Where shadows dance

Disillusioned I watch
With subdued mind
Insight of my inner self

Glowing embers
Breathing soft warm light
Into the cold night

Night call
Shatters the silence
Echoing through the darkness

Velvet black night
Creeps slowly through
The open window

The candle flame
Snuffed out by an icy breeze
To a wisp of grey curling smoke

Red hot embers
Turn to grey dust
Cold and lifeless

So I sit alone in the night
Until the defused light of dawn
Caresses my mellow eyes.

Marisa Greenaway

A Long Way Down

The brandishing beech is bold
As a mountain and brilliant green
As a peridot. I remember once
My cousin climbing up and up:
His father craning on the lawn
Advising caution.

The eager boy on the top boughs
Is a sad man. His father,
Who feared for him, shattered his world
Shook down his home, and no one ever
Has been able to put it
Together again.

Gillian Bence-Jones

That's Alf

His voice a little shaky.
His scalp is very flaky.

That's Alf

Fixes anything - hovers to old cars.
Never got any money always in bars.

That's Alf

Wears a grey jumper, always got a carrier bag.
Nicotine on his fingers stained by fags.

That's Alf

Always sniffing, always got a cold.
Brown frowny face, I reckon he's quite old.

That's Alf.

Hattie Boulding

ASHES TO ASHES

I watched her die in blue-white furnace flames,
it broke my heart to see them at her feet
as our photo aged to sepia in the heat.
Then an impish wind through heat cracks in the door
skittered her white ashes round the quarried floor,
soft-slurried now by probing winter rains.

Intimate of sky and winds our former house
gives up its mysteries, its memories:
our Bible, chronicling four centuries,
now hosts curled pages dry as autumn leaves.
On the blackened floor a stook of old corn sheathes
shelters one lone resident, a shy dormouse.

Stairs that reveal the timbered roof's in-fall
creak: no one is there. As I stand spellbound
a grey-white ghost floats, light as thistledown.
An inner truth tells me this cannot be
but remembrances in nature's inventory
can conjure visions thought beyond recall.

Set free I see her spectral shape dissolve:
a grey pall covers me like a nimbus cloud -
I become her ghost, she my gifted shroud.
Ashes to ashes: it is my time to go:
as I join her in a rainbowed afterglow
all life's unanswered questions then resolve.

Norman Meadows

High Rise Living

I've heard of high rise living,
up there in your penthouse suite,
tie adrift, shirt undone,
playing hard to get.
You have the whole world at your feet,
nothing to the right nor left,
and only God above.

You fly 'twixt Earth and Heaven,
in a cockpit cool as polished steel.
You're nicely oiled, wear purple shades,
and smell of class. The marble vestibule
throws back the tap of well-heeled shoes.
The latest hubs, like silver grapes,
lie throttled down below.

You deal in futures, so I hear,
both yours and mine no doubt.
Your salary, to match the stars,
breathes awesome mint, as sick as sin.
With bonus, your conversion
rises like the morning sun,
beyond the apparition of St Paul's.

After sweeping bargains from the city floor,
you slide like grease into a bath of foam.
Later, powder dry, you skim the polished pine,
and sink into a leather well.
Sculptures pose like gods. Chrome outshines
the heavens. Etchings hang like fruit
beyond the pale.

Under crystal glass, as cold as ice,
where time hangs on a pendulum of light,
a hawkish woman in a long black gown,
with shoulders bare, and moist red lips,
as open as a glass of wine,
will come for nothing,
other than a touch of gilt.

Afterwards, you dump the stars,
and wind up in the early hours,
drinking whisky with the heartless moon.
Upon a bearskin rug, a snow-white poodle, honed
to counterpoint, its pink gin tongue in cheek,
and slender legs in curly muffs,
is softly playing Bach.

Keith Shaw

THE WAR

The war seemed
To dominate
All of the news
We would watch
It on telly
Mornings and afternoons
I felt for the parents
Wives and girlfriends
Who were waiting
For news of their
Loved ones again
It's hard to imagine
How stressful it was
Although fighting wars
There is always a cause
I hope that it ends soon
Their heartache will pass
And they can share
Peace once again
With their love.

Jeanette Gaffney

WEEKEND TEARS

Time hangs heavy on my hands.
The ticking clock it dies away.
Weekend rain weeps sadly down.
I'm longing for the close of day.
My spirits low, weighed down with care
My thoughts go winging to the past
As memories come flooding back
Of all those things not meant to last.

My birthday is approaching fast.
I don't know where the years have gone
And each new wrinkle on my face
Simply makes me more forlorn.
I'm weary and weighed down with care.
I reach for you but you're not there.

Grey rain is lashing down on me
An echo of the way I feel.
The pressure of the past few weeks
Just makes each moment seem unreal.
As I grow weary with the years,
There's nothing left save weekend tears.

Rosemary Thomson

LOVER'S SOLILOQUY

When I wait for you at the door,
It is because I am afraid that I shall see you no more.
But when by chance I see you again -
Then I know the waiting was not in vain.

They say you should not emphasise
What goes on behind those eyes,
Those eyes so blue, yet soul like fire,
Could this not be called Desire?

Yes, it is hard to be patient and of good cheer,
When time can rob us of our fear,
The fear that all of life does pass too fast -
And nothing it would seem, was made to last.

It is true, I cannot lie,
That I am afraid to die.
For who can say what lies ahead?
When every breath is gone and we are dead.
Perhaps we float like in some dream,
But never to waken - too awful it must seem.

We have today, we have tomorrow.
Why should it end in grief and sorrow?
The Sun will still rise, the Moon will still wax and wane,
And you and I together shall remain.

Hilarie Grinnell

Pull Up A Chair

Let's sit in a circle holding hands
  And let our bodies do the talking.
If words come in a natural way
  Let's pass the message the voice controls,
Let's feel the warmth of someone there,
  Let's touch and hear. Come pull up a chair.
Let's cut out all the blaring sounds
  Created by machine mad men
Caught in a life of sealed souls
  And inanimated, graphic, patterned goals.
Let flow the vibes and naturally share.
  Come in my friend and pull up a chair.

Joan E Blissett

MAN AND TREE

Some trees
Lifespans are similar to man's,
Saplings grow, bear fruit
Produce hardy clan,
Suffer seasonal shake-ups,
Seasons serene,
When robust and rugged,
Part of the scene
As they grow older
Weakness appears,
Looking weather-beaten; strength
Starts to disappear.

Man and tree
Experience gales and
Tornadoes through years,
Ferreting those with feet of clay,
Weak and feeble blown to ground,
Returned again to Mother Nature,
Great statures laid low,
Ashes to ashes, earth to earth,
Man and tree echoed.

Hilary Jill Robson

ODE TO LAZE

Lazy, far too lazy, far too idle,
Don’t ask me.
Far too needful of relaxing,
Far too dodgeful of all taxing
Action that disrupts my lethargy.
I don’t run when I can sidle,
I make slothes look suicidal,
Vegetate with pride;
So don’t ask me.
Idle, far too idle, far too lazy.

Martin Choules

Cissbury Ring

One day I looked to Cissbury Ring
and saw her smiling face
it seemed she was inviting me
to feel her fond embrace.

I ambled up the gentle path
that led me through the trees -
the trees were all a'murmuring
responding to the breeze.

Then when I reached the ancient ring
that overlooks the sea
the skylarks with their swelling song
rose up to welcome me.

Just as an eagle on the heights
surveys his chosen land
I felt a sense of freedom - from
the countryside I scanned.

The Seven Sisters in the sun
enjoyed the evening light -
contrasting with the Sussex Weald -
a switchback gleaming white.

And looking west expectantly
across the hills of baize
I glimpsed the bashful Isle of Wight
veiled by a summer haze.

So if you're feeling down at heart
then please take this advice
go rest awhile on Cissbury Ring
and sample Paradise.

Jonathan Bryant

Movement

One ray of light pierces its way
through the shuttered window.
Within it, I can see
dust particles moving in the air.
They rise and dip,
dancing on a current
that I cannot feel.
I had thought my life
was completely still,
but now I see
that there is movement
all around me.
Time moves,
the air moves,
and dust moves.
It dawns on me
that eventually it will be
the movement of time
that will stir the air
where my dust will dance
in the light.
Only then, will I move again.

M M Graham

CRAZY

The mothers bask in the glory;
it sounds like a happy story.
Their children sit in disguise;
Mum doesn't see it as unwise.

One is two but already old;
vanity has entered the fold.
A beauty pageant winner;
so young there's something sinister.

She looks like a glamour model
who feels uneasy with it all.
She'll have to grow up one day.
Why does it have to be today?

Anthony Welsh

Nature's Call

Listen to nature's call
Snowflakes start to fall
Hear the wild winds roar

Chase the flowing rivers
Follow them to the sea
Listen to nature's call

Leaves fall from every tree
Branches waving frantically
Hear the wild winds roar

Onward the torrent rushes
Across pebbles and waterfall
Listen to nature's call

Passing under many bridges
Meandering along its way
Hear the wild winds roar

See the waters flowing
Past village, town and city
Listen to nature's call
Hear the wild winds roar.

John Edney

Broad Beans

I prepare the soil for their comfort,
I feed, protect and support them,
I set the scene for the seeds to swell
Snug inside their plump, green fingers.

Then I pounce.
I feel and squeeze the pods gently
Judging the moment to rip them from their stems.
I, who have nurtured them, do this.

Then sitting at ease in the sun
I tear open their flesh
And prise each perfect pearl
From its plush lined case.

I put aside these jewels
For further torment
And lightly toss away the skins,
The soft, green pelts.

I rise and plunge the naked
Little ones into boiling water
To prepare them for their final skinning,
The revealing of their bright, secret hearts.

Now exposed and vulnerable
They are anointed with hot oil
And sacrificed to our appetites
With ceremony and appreciation.

But who will forgive me?
Who will forgive me
For engaging their trust
Then betraying them so abominably?

Jean Fletcher

THE LENGTH OF COTTON THREAD

Silly things are promises we make as if we know
What life will deal our way and in what ways we are to grow
I didn't know that crystal broke as dreams shattered worth
Nor that cats scratch your tongue as utterances rush forth

You never told me what it was I ought to know
Nor that I am, I am, and not what you did sow
I told myself your thoughts from what you gave me as a child
You told me I was not the thing that I would hope abide

Do I love this child or am I nought but cotton thread
To wind around your finger and in knots to live in dread
My edges they are frayed but you tell me that I'm new
But the loom broke long ago and I make do with what I do

I see that I shall have to make decisions I don't like
I see you do that too, but you say you cope with life
It doesn't seem to me that it's worth is what you get
And I wonder at injustice o'er this length of cotton thread.

Maggie Jones

WAR-TIME CHILDHOOD

We lived in other people's houses, Mum and I;
Some untidy, others neat unto obsession,
Some smelled of drains and damp, some smelled of carrot pie.
Most felt cold, for coal was minuscule of ration.

Mrs P had rules, our ration books collected.
She gave us potatoes and vegetable stew.
At night to air-raid shelter, warm beds neglected,
Where beetles, musty smells, hard bunks and comforts few.

At dawn the 'all clear' sounded; candles waxy smell.
Where's the cat? Will the house be there still? we wondered,
Or would it all be rubble, a tangled heap, a hell?
(The sweet shop across the road, a bomb had plundered.

The baby's cot suspended from the bedroom floor.
The owner's private lives exposed to public gaze.
Hanging from its hinge was a crazy, drunken door.
And still, o'er all hung a dusty, desolate haze.)

Today, our school playground was a pile of rubble,
The gates were locked, with notice, I, too young to read.
No school, no jubilation, no mum to cuddle.
She worked on munitions. I alone. None took head.

A searing pain, one day, bore into ear and head.
'To hospital!' A cot with bars my prison made.
The nurses sang their wartime songs. My heart was lead.
At night they ran with cots on wheels. 'Quick!' Matron bade.

In lifts they took the cots, into the depths of earth.
The caves beneath are safe from bombs, my nurse offered.
To soothe my anxious cries, but stroking there was dearth.
Even Mum could but steal a touch, fingers proffered.

Children *can* recover. We play on playground ice.
The vigorous run up, then, glide, waving arms wide.
Crisp, cold air, rushing through my hair, burns eyes and face.
A hole in sole of shoe, no clothing coupons! . . . 'Hide!'

Pam Kearsley

The Good Shepherd

On a craggy hill a straggle of sheep
Huddled together, restless in sleep
In a futile endeavour to keep themselves warm
Seeking comfort and warmth from a rough winter's storm.

Low in the sky heavy thunder clouds break
Sending to earth sleeting rain in their wake
Forking of lightning vibrant and deep
Casting flashes and shadows on the flock as they sleep.

Outlining each rock, every cranny and nook
Sparse clumps of gorse, and a small winding brook
As the cauldron of witches shrieking its song
Wailing and bubbling as it tumbles along.

Away in the distance, a flicker of light
A 'will-o'-the wisp' on a storm sodden night.
The faithful old shepherd has traversed alone
Leaving the warmth and the comfort of home.

Deep in the valley his cottage lies there
Loves his animal friends with devotion and care
A life he has known since he was a lad
Religiously followed in the steps of his dad.

Tending his flock in this wild raging storm
To do what he can to keep them from harm
For one who had strayed its bleating now ceased
As he brings back to shelter this wandering beast.

The storm has subsided, he is ready for bed
Contented to know they are watered and fed
For this trusty old shepherd constant vigil will keep
To be ever mindful in the care of his sheep.

Barbara Davies

FAIRGROUND

What's that noise and what's that sound
It's coming from the fairground
Lots of music and plenty of chatter
It's on the park so it doesn't matter
Voices screaming loud and clear
Coming from the waltzes here
A big wheel going round and round
Dodgem cars with a thumping sound
Helter skelter with straw mats
A ghost train with flying bats
Hook a duck a prize every time
Slot machines all in a line
A carousel and a pirate ship
Coconut shy and lucky dip
Hot dog stands and candy floss too
Plenty to eat and lots to do
Flashing lights all around
So much fun at the fairground.

Tina Davis

STRESS

Space,
Give me space,
To breathe the fresh air,
In solitude without stress,
To get away,
From the pressures of life,
The twisting knife,
The hemming me in,
Controlling restraints,
The mess.

The throb at my brain,
The tick at my heart,
Like an animal caged,
I rant and rage,
I pace about,
Go to and fro,
Feeling confined,
Life passing me by,
Until the day I die?

Ann G Wallace

I Am Not Proud

I watched war's suffering on TV's screen
and felt the agony of families
where death had struck, homes blown to smithereens,
lives lost and pain of ghastly injuries . . .
joined in the prayers that armies would retreat
and cried with people wailing in the street.

Should I feel proud my country was involved
when soldiers and civilians died in vain?
Was this the best way problems could be solved
causing the innocent such grief and pain?
When war is over, we help pay the cost
but there is no repayment for lives lost.

The sun shines while our country wears a cloud . . .
I am not proud!

Joy Saunders

To Emma
My Daughter

No words can ever really say
What my daughter means to me.
So beautiful, so funny, her individuality.
The way she looks upon her world
With an optimistic smile.
Her very sensitive nature
Her fashionable style.
Her laughter warms me always.
Deep into my soul.
Her lovely blue and sparkling eyes
That make my heart feel whole.
Her bubbly excitement
When she looks ahead.
To all the plans completed
Then does something else instead.
Now a bright young woman
With a full life of her own.
She's still my baby in my heart
Still lighting up my home.

W A Ronayne

OUR MOST PERFECT MOMENT

(For Russ)

You're mine all mine this moment,
the closest we can be,
I look up from below you,
you're deep inside of me.

Your kisses long and linger,
your taste so strong and sweet,
you bite my neck then look up
then resume your lover's beat.

As we move together,
your thrusts become intense,
your breathing's getting deeper,
your moans arouse my sense.

Rhythmic sways, sensual music,
your eyes meet mine we melt
into each other's psyche,
a soaring moment felt.

I lift my hips to meet yours,
the climax moment nears.
You're looking down in ecstasy,
your look dissolves my fears.

As we shake together,
pure synchronicity,
'I love you more than ever,'
you come deep inside of me.

You're mine all mine this moment,
a tear tumbles down my face.
You're held here within me,
a perfect special place.

Suzie Burton

Pet Loves And Hates

Rosehips and tulips, fruit without pips,
late evening sea trips, and insects 'non-nip'
taps that don't drip, and afternoon kips.

Husbands who wash up and 'don't' leave it neat,
loo roll users, who leave only one sheet.
Village and town, without 'bobby' on beat.

Half of the readers will think, 'yes' that's me.
The other half say, 'I don't quite agree'
isn't it good that we're not all the same,
because if we were, they'd have no one to blame!

Beryl F Lenihan

I Live In Cardboard City

I live in cardboard city
Which is near paper town,
The scenery is gloomy
As they have knocked the houses down.
I haven't got a window
As that would make a draft,
I haven't got a door
Which makes the postman laugh.
I don't get many letters
As my address is not well known,
But I do have a garden
Which is weedy and overgrown.
So if you want to write to me
A letter cheerful and witty,
Just address it to box number two
To a place called cardboard city.

Stephanie Lynn Teasdale

WAR AND PEACE

Across the street, beyond the square
The bomb for Palestine met you
A Jewish sister, twin and friend
Rogue Chance had cast his die.

Your husband could not speak for tears
His room an empty shrine
When you lay cold beneath the sheet
Your hair like autumn leaves.

Yet Grief today an alien stands
Imposter, stranger, waif.
For round a statue strewn with flowers
Lithe dancers clap, musicians sway.

The victors chant their hollow cant
As you lie in your grave.
I weep in vain, your voice is lost
And Israel's crown is won?

Anne Gaelan

Lasting Love

In that long hot golden summer of our youth
Love stepped in and caught us by surprise,
As hand in hand beneath those cobalt skies
We dreamed together, from the world aloof.
Young and untried our love yet made us proof
Against fortune's knocks, bound us with silken ties,
Assured each new day a glorious sunrise
And blossomed into a rich rewarding truth.
Through the years our love has kept us strong,
Its passion cooled now to a gentle heat,
But still those ties of silk hold fast
Still each to the other does belong.
Like one combined our separate hearts do beat
They will continue so until the last.

Frances Marie Cecelia Harvey

My Nose Out Of Joint

I drape my blue-grey silhouette
sphinx-like on the brink of peace,
distinguished, ornamental cat
prone to weird laments' release.
Insipid pity I despise,
I am *ousted* from my throne;
well you may peer into my eyes,
seek my soul, aloof, alone.
Distinct is carved my regal frame
and a scream escapes my maw.
I shall not answer to my name -
now my owner's feeding *four!*
So delicate my fur, so svelte
yet I bristle with disdain
for never have I ever felt
such inordinate sheer pain.
Four sets of orbs my own replace,
topaz, emerald they gleam,
rifling territorial space,
gluttonously supping cream.
My mistress, she may holler loud
her stentorian command;
I care not - I am grossly proud,
on my dignity I stand
for, once she worshipped at my shrine,
raison d'etre I was he.
Forgive, forgive my banshee whine,
blame her infidelity.

Ruth Deviat

Escape From Bank Holiday

The reed beds are restless with riffling and rustling
As wind works his will on this North Norfolk coast.
The mud creeks are crowded with wading birds, bustling;
Their haunting cries echo like howls from some ghost.

The sea is far out as the birds feed, unceasing.
This glistening mud offers gourmet delights.
They know that the next tide will finish their feasting.
Then they will soar seawards in effortless flight.

The pure air refreshes; perceptions are shifting;
The scent of the turning tide tempers the mood.
Gone is the ghostliness; spirits are lifting.
Elation flows in with the in-surging flood.

Carol Burton

The Dance Of The Clouds

The cumuli gather without apologies or regret
As the lord of the wind does bequeath
And thus the clouds move like pawns on a board
Taking their shape within an ominous mass
The wind changes attire from a nice sedate breeze
Changing slowly into a premeditated rage
Flexing its muscles in a deteriorating mood
Evoking the forces of nature to arms
The clouds march together in their military grey
Swollen and pregnant with the burden of rain
Upon a mindless foray without honour or guilt
Blighting the embers of the civilised mind
Darker and darker the invading mass grows
Smothering the light from the sociable sun
The smell of expectancy does perfume the air
Until the patience of the burden relents
The clouds start to dance, the thunder explodes
The air roars with the tantrums of Thor
Lightning sets fire to the spite laden sky
Stabbing the Earth with its pre-ordained curse
Buildings do tremble and animals run scared
People cower 'neath the safety of fear
The sea delivers contempt upon the innocent ships
Battering the coastline with its unyielding abuse
Through its raw passion, anger, malice and hate
Mercy is lost in the torrential bleak rain
All thee shall see is the dance of the clouds
Seething across the intoxicated sky.

David Bridgewater

LESS

You don't know what's inside of me,
I'm judged by what you hear and see.
Because I smile and nod my head
And don't react to what is said,
Doesn't mean that on defection
I haven't noticed the deflection,
And in doing so, think less of you.

Don't think that you can be unkind
And I'll dismiss it from my mind.
Inside of me I'm quite aware
Of snide remarks I too could share,
But then I'm glad that I hold back,
What good is going down that track?
Would only make me just like you.

And so I smile and nod my head
And speak of different things instead.
'I love your dress, your hairstyle too,
And don't you suit that shade of blue?'
And then I go and make some tea
While knowing, deep inside of me,
There'll be less of me to give to you.

Harriet-Ann

I'll Always Remember Paris

I shall always think of Paris, it gave me the will to live
To realise you're all mixed up, a life with so much to give
Virtually torn in pieces, till a friend offered me an advance
Take a break to the 'City of Paris', for it will give you the chance
Opportunities don't come often, rare like a moment in time
Going to this magical city, for a vacation was a dream divine
Holidaymakers flock in droves, to relax and take in the sites
Paris is like a magnet, masses of pinkish lights
Stretching for miles on boulevards, far as the eye can see
These Parisian nights and all their charm, leaves only a memory
In France they sing and partisan, with lives so sublime
Cafes filled with tourists, waiters serving wine
The landscape is a work of art, surrounded with gardens so neat
Looming tall the Eiffel Tower, lovers come to meet
Though my stay was short, my life is coming back
I sense I'm a different person, I feel I am on track
A desperate soul it rescued, forever I'll be thankful for this
England may be my country, I'll always feel that way about Paris.

J R H Graham

PERHAPS

Imagine our world,
Filled with love not hate.
Imagine an abundance of food,
Shared amongst each city, country and state.

Imagine one season.
The warmth of summer all the time.
Imagine no criminals,
And a society free from crime.

Imagine no drug dealers
And the lives this would save.
Imagine no peer pressure,
And no illegal raves.

Imagine cures for all illness,
No more sickness or death.
Imagine future generations,
Not taking a last breath.

Imagine eternity,
With no care of time elapsed.
Imagine living in peace.
Maybe one day we might . . . perhaps.

Anne Leeson

INVASION

Maybugs fall down the chimney,
Spiders scuttle round the bath,
Earwigs creep across the carpet,
Ants march up the path.
Insectivorous intruders,
Creepy-crawlies galore,
Keep invading No. 24!

Sue Cann

If Sunshine Could Be Bottled

If sunshine could be bottled what a fortune I would make.
I know that it would sell - oh how much money I could take!
It makes the whole day better, even if it started bad,
For sunshine lifts your whole mood even if you're feeling sad.

Not only does it warm your heart, your step will have more spring.
It's funny what a difference to your feelings it can bring.
Things don't look half as bad when there's that brightness in the sky.
How sad that on the weather we just really can't rely!

Tina Dolby

'POETA' (M)

*('The gender of a Latin noun by meaning, form or use is shown.'
- Kennedy Revised Latin Primer)*

Try it like this: read the poem
once from start to finish -
you should be able to tell
whether man, or woman, wrote it.

Does it work to impress you as
by the better craftsman
in the maternal tongue; or
simply unfold, and undress you?

Picture the scarlet woodpecker,
tense pose fixed to the bole,
drumming up his distant love
in reverberating salvoes.

Compare how the eye may be led
to subtle eddyings
of water crowsfoot from where
dart grayling to sip early nymphs.

Sometimes the lasered cyphers of
sunstruck heliotrope
dazzle the mind's optic nerve
and reflect only zigzag light.

That's when shade nurtures the seedling,
the wand kindles a fuse.
Suddenly, there's a figure
dancing like Botticelli's Spring!

John Weston

TWIGS

The badgers
forage by eve
like little lawn mowers
the sound down,
gamely feasting on
quietness
until wild danger
tramps by . . .

Suddenly! Heart beats
like an Olympic sprint . . .

They race off
and I am left to chew.

Lee McLaughlin

Island Paradise

Take an island,
Hide it away
In secret solitude,
Give it sun,
Infuse deep colour,
Scallop the west
With shell-sand beaches,
Breathtaking brilliancy
Of white and turquoise,
Fringe the east
With beaded necklace,
A filigree of shining rock
Set with pools of blue,
Drop a snaking ribbon road
Round humpy hillocks,
Scatter white houses
On sheep-mown lawns,
Place paddling cattle
Mid flower-rich machair,
Inject a curlew call,
An oystercatcher cry,
Float a distant boat
On mirror sea,
Project voices to shore
In utter stillness.

Take this island,
Make a vision of peace
To bank in subconsciousness
For recall at any time,
Vivid in the mind's eye,
Intimate yet infinite,
Surface calm belying
Underlying restlessness,
Overwhelming beauty
Hard to bear alone,

Diluted in solitude
Yet hard to share,
Heightened in secrecy,
Heart-aching in love,
Emotions merge
In seascape atmosphere,
Surge in waves together,
One in being
On this island.

Janet Forrest

The Little Things . . .

In the garden, 'The oasis of love and care',
I missed you again.
The fish in the pond
And the birds in their songs,
Felt my sorrow.
And the palms with their shadow
And the flowers with their scents,
Felt my sorrow.

But in the fountain the water drips told me
You are in my heart.
It's only my hands miss to hold yours,
My skin misses to sense yours.
My ears, when words are echoing.
My lips when air rushing through.
My feet when touching the ground.
My nose when thousand fragrances float.
My arms when find you not.
The empty chair and cup and shoes . . .
Only the little things are reminding me of you my love.

Clarissa Beöthy

BERSHAM COLLIERY

Each day, at dawning light,
I drop into the dark.
Down and down, down I go.
The earth is home to me.

First, a detour for a smoke.
Woodbine and a single match,
Heading for the winding -
Wheel. Submerge in the shaft.

Blackbird black envelops.
I grasp my pick, bend my back
And subjugate the coal.
'Snappin' comes. I eat the dust.

My lips are caked with grime.
Water tastes as good as wine.
It's nectar to my throat.
Pass the hours, I sweat and toil.

The day is gone. All my strength
Escapes into the world.
First a bath and I go,
In haste, towards my home.

Laura P Williams

Joyce

The happiest woman I ever did meet
Wore floppy slippers on stocking feet
Her hair in pinned rollers, on her cardy a stain
Outside toilet with inside rain

The walls were wonky, chimneys clogged full
Photos of old friends, knitting and wool
Windows untended, dust of her life
Photos of children, and husband and wife

Chintz and doilies, pictures askew
Grandchildren smiling, the only things new
Painted plates on shelving high
A husband a memory, a time that's gone by

Hands of her labour, wrinkled and old
Eyes full of wisdom, stories untold
Fragile her time, her future just so
Until her reunion with husband to go

Each line tender, carved by the past
Soft voice so gentle, kind to the last
She just a flicker, in time with her kin
Each heart touched by love that's within

Her children adore her, her grandchildren too
Touching the lives of all that she knew
A treasure so valuable, how do you cope?
Giver of life, mother of hope.

Shirley Cawte

Changing Fashions

Those holiday postcards in a bungle stored
A precious collection of memories held tight
Clamped altogether with a coloured cord

Messages of 'arrived here safe and sound'
'The digs' are good and there's plenty to eat
Envoking the happiness that seems to abound

Perhaps the seaside splendours of yesteryear
With children's smiling faces and donkey rides
When bathing beauties under big sun hats appear

Now the mobile users seem to be in their place
When that 'wsh u wr hr' is punched out in text
No time for the well-loved communication's face

So this is a poetic ode to that holiday card
Of a one, once highly favoured by the masses
Yet text is now, forever is the postcard bard.

Octavia Hornby

REQUIEM

Music bringing back the memories of times gone by
The feeling and the sense, the when, where and why?
Like a feather on the breeze and sifting sands of a beach
Music bringing back the memories of times now out of reach

When other dreams were dreamt and other people longed for
When other pains were strong and pleasures seemingly more
The choices, the snapshots, the censored, the forgotten
So what fruits of now will fall rotten?
What flowers will grow and blossom . . . ?

Stuart Davey

To Elizabeth Catlow And Her Fiance

From pledges union two souls be married,
When false impediments confounded be,
Were love's token rings in honour carried,
Are one signet bound in eternity.
So two star'd lovers kiss with lips intent,
Made content by their love for each other,
Which love in crystal raise does augment,
A revelry of belles with studs cover,
What fair possessing fare can excel this,
This passing scene of surpassing gladness,
This summer fate made summer by love's bliss,
This lover's knot tied tight in happiness,
Thus by love's giving and receiving oath
Is love sworn fair and sworn is love to both.

Barry Bradshaigh

Playing In Time

Two
rhythmic
sleek dots run
bars of shining
sea

One
brooding
small prelude
to tempests of salt

We
attuned
walk wet sand
recapture lost
airs.

P P Crittenden

Dental Check

He looked then smiled into my mouth
Then stretched it from both north and south
Like Captain Blood he took his hook
And in my mouth he took a look

Do not worry it will not hurt
Those four words made me alert
For I myself felt very small
He was large and very tall

Around my mouth he went with ease
Turned on his drill just to tease
My heart at that point fled away
Does he pay I heard him say

Not much for me to do today
A spit and polish shall we say
Just to keep the plaque at bay
Not to worry there's no decay

My legs like jelly tried to stand
The nurse gave me a gentle hand
Then to my senses I was found
This check had cost me sixty pounds.

J A Vessey

CATS' EYES

Always there, dutiful at night,
Gold sequins on black velvet,
In pairs, jewelled eyes gleaming bright
On a long, concrete carpet.

Powerless, yet so powerful,
Reliant on headlights' gleam
To activate their helpful glow,
Light the way with steady beam.

Twentieth century genius mimics
Nocturnal, feline features,
Illuminating paths ahead,
Cars indebted to creatures!

Power failures does not affect them,
They crouch in tarmac blackness
Ready to glow 'purr'fectly like
Minute beacons in darkness.

Only dawn can switch off the eyes,
They never tire! Tyres, millions
By day squash these sleeping glow-worms,
Push them into oblivion.

Next night they all bounce back alert
In their golden sequinned strips,
Though transport treats them very rough
Constant vigil never slips!

Pat Heppel

Hues And Cries

Shuffling through the crisp carpet of golden leaves,
Like a child, splashing with its first pair wellingtons,
I trust no one will spy my infantile pleasure.

I shiver as the watery sun,
Near washed away by winter's keenness,
Attempts a weak smile through the mist.

The mellow golden hues of the lingering leaves
Serve to remind me of summer's goodness.
But those cascading to their demise
Bring thoughts of snow showers to come,
And the departing days of autumn.

Diane Bowen

Beasts Of Freedom

The harsh wind wails,
As the ghost ship sails.
Strange screams vibrate,
Beasts of freedom wait:
Feasting on fears,
Drinking from the vine of tears.
Air and fire are as one,
Singing the Earth's song.
Water is flowing under the moon,
Broken flowers are trying to bloom,
Naked bodies lie on the sea,
Beasts of freedom, killers of the free.

Julius Howard

The Robber's Apprentice

A hot day's walking, a throat so dry - then he saw an inn close by
The quiet as he reached the door - rough faces turned to him he saw
Why there's young Jack don't I know you? Just one friend among that crew?
Recalling then that shifty face - full of art and lacking grace
Jack lad don't be scorning me - remember our village by the sea?
He had been warned while still a lad - to steer away from one so bad,
But ale has ways to loose a tongue - friends it makes while foes among
Sit you down Jack don't fret - come take with me another wet
Rich we'll be Jack without fail - when we robs the Royal Mail
By yonder road they stand and wait - to stop the coach and seal its fate
A pistol gives him courage new - the deed ere long to carry through
Horses neighing from afar - the posthorn sounds a loud hurrah
Iron rims crunch upon the road - hooves slip and spark a heavy load
The nearby hill has slowed them yet - an urgent cry come Jack get set
Into the path of horses bold - a voice rings out coachman hold
Toward him now a pistol turns - he sees the flame then feels the burns
Well done my friend from in the coach - it's the chief thief taker Captain Roach
While laying in his lonely call - he hears his mother's words full well
Always do your daily work - have naught to do with those that shirk
His new friend gone with a jingling purse - come to this for a dry throat's curse,
He sees a face the beady eye - it is the hangman come to spy,
A piece of rope his claim to fame - yet ne'er recalled the other's name
On the morrow hangman grim - will leave his mother to weep for him.

John Of Croxley

WRONG NUMBER

My hair was getting far too long
Need a trim and have it gone,
Phone hairdresser on that day
Answering machine began to play,
Leave a message I will get back
Later on my brain I rack,
For on the phone was a man,
It was not my hairdresser, Ann,
A gentleman on phone line sang
'Never cut hair before, but dang,
I'll have a go if you want me to
Called you back but I'm not who
You really wanted that's for sure,
Phone Ann and she will have the cure,
You phoned the wrong number dear,
I can't help you I fear.'
We said goodbye and all is well,
I'll make sure on a future spell,
Eyes will be fixed upon the numbers,
Won't make any more of these blunders.

J Naylor

Good Friends

What start to the new year, what an end to the last.
So look to the future, not back at the past.
Although I'm in plaster up to my thigh
I can hop on my good leg! How lucky am I?
I could have broken both legs then where would I be?
I should still have my friends popping in to see me.
The phone calls, enquiries, all wishing me well,
So many good friends, too many to tell.
All their good wishes and sympathy too,
And my doggie walkers, especially you,
A big thank you to all who showed that you care,
Thank you everyone everywhere,
Especially Elizabeth, my very best friend,
For cooking and nursing and helping me mend.

Irene Keeling

A Day At The Seaside

Children playing happily on a beach
Having a ball and such jolly good fun
While older folks are just lying around
Soaking up the warm summer sun.

Blow-up crocodiles covered in sand
Punch and Judy are doing their bit
The donkeys trudging up and down
Looking tired, but they're really a hit.

Deckchair attendants bustle about
Ice cream sellers plying their trade
Sandcastles of every shape and size
Fall apart while others are made.

Parasols, deckchairs and windbreaks
All flapping in the onshore breeze
Knotted hankies and kiss-me-quick hats
Worn by fathers and mothers to tease.

Open-topped buses and silent trams
Wend their way along their tracks
While nans and gramps sit on the prom
Eating chips, dressed in see-through macs.

Everyone's making the most of the day
Because reality comes back with a jerk
Remembering that today is a Sunday
And tomorrow we're all back at work.

John William Osland

I REMEMBER THE DAY

Rare snowfall spelled us
into children. Pink, round,
snotty grinnings in fat-boy clothes.
Rushing over the downs,
kicking through the white plain
with all the glee of newborn lambs.
Eyes, wide-surprised as natives
of equatorial zones.
Later, in a twist of physics, the cold
proved getting warm a heat.

Now, years gone through the burning
ring and the slow spread of continents
separate us with a quantum quirk:
the further apart we are
the closer we've become.
I have all the snow I can eat,
up to my lashes in it and you,
as you've said in letters, you
scan each winter sky
for squalls.

Bruce McRae

The Power And The Glory

There comes a time in one's life, they say,
When by order of mystery in life's calling
There is a moment that a path will lay,
As one treads it takes on the means of falling.

This is when that light gives faith, leading kindly,
And in one's heart, takes over.
Look into the eyes of one, who lifts the fallen blindly,
To place one on a bank of four-leaf clover.

When love has cured all ills and mended the soul,
All ills are gone, one feels fulfilled.
Take flight, dear one, quenched by nature's bow,
Faith returns like fresh soil been tilled.

John Clarke

ELVIS IN PERSPECTIVE

I remember Elvis well,
I had his hairstyle set in gel -
or Brylcream as it was for me
and took on his identity
and that of Dean and also Cliff -
though only his tsunami quiff.
I even had my hair blacked -
Or indigoed, to be exact.

I didn't see the real Elvis,
only the gyrating pelvis
and sneer that he'd begun to lose
in the movie 'GI Blues'.
Behind the scenes there was another,
a food-junkie and his mother,
a Jesus-freak and getting fatter;
by that time, though, it didn't matter.

Richard Livermore

Coming Home

Don’t go just yet, please stay.
The sun is out and you know you love its warmth.
Lying here - face upturned,
eyes moving in answer to our voices -
we tell you our news in the brightness of day.
You do not answer.
Your eyes just flicker.

They can’t help you anymore.
There seems little they can do
but we don’t want you staying
with strangers as your friends.
We smile at you.
You do not answer.
Your eyes just flicker.

Outside your room for two are
dusty double-decker buses and high-rise flats.
A world away from the world you knew.
We glance over, hopeful for recognition.
You do not answer.
Your eyes just flicker.

Though your days ahead may be short,
we want you out of here
to kindly faces, pavements lined with blossom.
The comforting nearness of the church you love.
You make a little sound. We look up hopefully.
You do not answer.
Your eyes just flicker.

The day of moving you arrives.
Cautiously and gently they transport you to your home.

They place you carefully in bed, smooth your pillows
and stroke your head.
Your eyes flicker, they open
and we smile!

Lynn Craig

TRAVELLING LINES

How can I start this
I just don't know
In a prose or rhyming form,
Which way shall I go?

Sat on a table,
On a chair,
On your knee
That blank piece of paper
Looks up eagerly.

Fill me with words, it says,
To light up a day
Fill me with couplets, pentameters -
Whatever - just do it
Sometime today?

Irratic written form.
A content that's new
Write something different,
Something that's true.

So for all those struggling
Moments out there,
Here's a new rhyme
To help you prepare.

For whatever you face
In your travels with lines,
Remember your thoughts
Will live beyond times.

E Di-Marcello

Across The Frontier

Across the frontier I could not speak the language.
I said nothing meaningful.
Silence became my language.
Back in my country in my native village
I could say nothing meaningful.
My heart, weary from despair and hope,
Anguish and joy, learned to wait patiently
For the birth of a new language.
There are many countries, but one sky, one life.

Angela Matheson

Seasons

Sometimes the stresses and strife
We all have to face in everyday life
Make me feel blue and down
And my face wears a frown,
Then no matter what season of year
I remember so many things so dear.

The first spring flowers
The Lord in His infinite power
Sends us free of charge
So that no matter how small or large
We can all enjoy them
From petal to stem.

Summer, with warm long days
That pass in a beautiful haze
Children playing on the beach
Then the tide's long arms reach
To wash the sandcastles away
So the children can build again another day.

Then the days begin to shorten
And before we know it, it's autumn
The fall of the golden leaves
So that bare and empty are the trees
Bonfire night and fireworks crack
Standing by the fire, warming my back.

With the snow comes the winter's chill
Dark cold nights, frosty and still
And during this season our Lord Jesus was born
Hence with this birth a new age dawned.
All in all these seasons remind me, no matter how down I feel,
Jesus is working in my life, He's alive, He's real!

Wendy Rennison

Sober Ring

The band stays on
Around her finger, wrapped so snug and smooth
A shining cut
The finest swathe through flesh, as if to prove
Their proper selves.

He used to drink
The madness sucked them both to fantasies
And high spirits
Ravaged her like his infidelities
When love was neat.

She's fair, but dull
Preserving beauty and euphoria,
The wedding's point
He thought he'd stop the life draining from her
In one thin place.

He did think once
Far from inebria, he planned this coup
But will is lost
To solve snowballing problems, they made two
One-way tickets.

The future's glow
On wagons to Nirvana, pales in shame
Against the wild
Of days when alcohol fuelled passion's flames
In Las Vegas.

Serena Shores

AROUND THE CORNER

You've made your plans, your hopes are high
But beware, for tomorrow disaster may be nigh.
A pattern repeated as well we all know
For to achieve our aim it's oft touch and go.
Just when success is in your sight
Doubts loom large and give you a fright.
As chance steps into alter your lot
With nary a regard for your original plot.
Doom and gloom may not inevitably follow an upset plan
For unexpected fortune can smile on any man.
We are all pawns in the clutch of fate
'Til finally we reach the heavenly gate.

Allen Jessop

THE ARTIST

He sets up his easel and sketches
On a hilltop above the town,
The artist doesn't rush what he's doing,
Creating the scenery around.

A church with its spire he starts sketching,
With a farm in the distance he adds,
Adjusting here and there with his rubber,
Enjoying the talent he has.

Then with his palette and paints he mixes,
Putting fluffy white clouds in the sky,
Four or five sheep in the churchyard,
With children playing nearby.

A fox and rabbits are then added,
Hedges and trees then appear,
Then some flowers to add colour,
With birds nesting quite near.

Sitting back - has he finished?
He checks to make sure it's complete,
There's just one more details he missed,
As he spies two men on a seat.

Trish Wright

TEENAGE TEARAWAY

I'm the mother of a teenage tearaway
Undisciplined, untidy and rude
She's tall and thin like a model
She's always picking at her food

She stops out all night with wild friends
Though I say, 'Please be home by eleven'
When I ask her what she's been doing
She says I treat her like a child of seven

I am told that this is a passing phase
She'll grow out of it all one day
That's little consolation to me right now
When all I can feel is dismay

I try to sit and watch the television
Enjoy the radio or a good book
Only to keep wondering where she is
How I wish I could go out and look

Like so many mums before me
I try to pretend that all is well
Twenty-past one, she's forgotten her key again
I'm jolted from my worries by the bell!

Barbara Manning

The Pages Of Life

The pages of life keep on turning,
As we write out a message each day,
Some pages are full of sweet laughter,
But others we would throw right away.

How oft do we write lovely pages,
Of deeds that are kind and well meant,
But in others our words and our actions,
Hurt more than we ever have dreamt.

As we write out the pages of history,
May our lives uplift and transform
The sorrowing, depressed and forsaken,
And give them new faith and new dawn.

May the pages reflect the dear Saviour,
Whose life in us we relive,
And bring by the Spirit to others
The love and forgiveness He gives.

R Baker

MAGICAL ENTERPRISE

I see, I know, I hear it all
I see, I know, I feel
I've seen the magic enterprise
So I know the magic's real

I know it's real with deep emotion
I feel the magic in my heart
I hold onto love with deep devotion
And never will we part

I've seen the light, I've seen the great
I feel a shining light around me
I no longer need investigate
As the magic does surround me

I feel the tingles in my soul
I feel my dancing feet
I feel the sun, the love that's whole
I feel the blessed heat

I feel the blood flow through my veins
I feel the shine within my eyes
I know the magic's here again
I've seen the magic enterprise

I've sensed the space
Dynamic power
I feel euphorical and great
Nothing shall be sour

I feel my heart pump every beat
I feel the rise and fall of air
I taste the magic that is sweet
I sense it everywhere

I feel my eyelids flutter
I feel the blood wash over muscle
I feel like melting butter
Into a heated happiness

I feel the tiny molecules
Of the magic yet to rise
I feel atomic, euphoric and free
I've seen the magic enterprise.

Janine Erline Griffiths

LAMENT OF AN AGENCY STUD

I never thought the time would come
that now has come to pass,
when like a worn-out thoroughbred
they've put me out to grass.

Schoolmates first noticed in the showers
I was indeed well-hung -
enough to frighten any girl
remotely highly strung.

With my raunchy reputation
I laid about the town.
My credentials were accepted,
a Don Juan of renown.

A regular Casanova,
entirely conscience-free,
I turned to roaming far and wide
across both land and sea.

Next, I took to adult filming,
as birds take to the air;
had leading ladies by the score,
some fully clothed, some bare.

Well past my sell-by date, I'm now
the butt of pious scorn.
It's doubly tough for such as me,
a one-time king of porn.

Terence Reid

DREAMBOAT

Joyously she rides the waves as in a distant dream
Her sleek bows cutting through the surging sea
Behind her is a wake of frothing cream
The open sea ahead is wild and free

Where the wind should take her she will fly
To distant lands so very far away
To islands which beyond horizons lie
Amid the rainbows in the flying spray

My dreamboat sailing on forever more
Skimming over waves of creamy white
In dreams I sail with you to distant shores
But dreams fade with the morning light.

Joan M Jones

DAYDREAMS

If only man would learn to share
his riches, discipline himself to spare
a fraction of the wealth he gains.
Maybe no child would tug distressed
and hungry at its mother's empty breast,
or scavenge in the dust for grain.
But men, preoccupied by selfish greed
with hearts unmoved by urgent need
feel no responsibility to feed
the weak and poor.

If only man would judge by deed
and word instead of colour, race or creed.
Suspicions crush and trust renew;
maybe nations would discover
they are no different from each other
black or white, Christian or Jew.
But men accustomed to depravity
indifferent to sanity
must demonstrate their inhumanity
to man once more.

If only man would learn to show
compassion, allow sympathy to grow
and understanding replace blame.
For men would then renounce the right
to vengeance, no more violence incite
or dark hostility inflame.
But feuds endure and conflicts rarely cease,
men cannot seem to live in peace.
Incessantly the cries increase,
'To war! To war!'

Sylvia Reader

It Was Not Murder

No it was not murder he had in mind.
It was not lust had he in his sad heart?
But it was low that foul committed start.
It was not virtuous. That glad unkind
Event bordered on gluttony dined.
There was space in darkness his soul's great part
The embrace of evil. He smiled the art
Of innocence. He cut and cut the find
Laughed as wounds became unbearable.
He thought of cartoons. The tears ran too raw
Down his cheeks. He ripped. He tore too stable
The frenzy. Micky Mouse ran he went 'Haw
Haw.' He cleaved the head from the badly-
Maimed torso with gust sawed madly.

Edmund Saint George Mooney

PEACEFUL

Ducks were swanning, carefree,
on the swiftly flowing river
and swans were lying, lazy,
on the bank.
Seagulls were busy,
screeching, high above them,
and a cat was crouching, wary,
by a puddle where it drank.

Tree reflections shimmered
on the surface of the water,
and the sun played hide-and-seek
between the clouds.
Serenity seems possible
when nature paints her pictures,
and a calmness waits for you and I
a brief walk from the crowds.

Ted Harrison

THE SORCERER'S DREAM

If I was just a sorcerer,
I'd wear a pointy hat,
Have ancient rings upon my hand
And own an old black cat.
Perhaps a magic wizard
And my flowing robe would be
Embroidered with the stars and moon
And all the galaxies.

My hands so long and bony
And a wart upon my nose,
A magic glint within my eye
To cast upon my foes.
My castle would be made of stone,
Built on a mountain high,
With drawbridge, moat and turrets
That so pierced the night-time sky.

A stairway deep into the earth,
Of age no one could tell,
A cauldron in the cellar
Where I go to cast my spells.
And passageways beneath the ground,
A maze of many rooms,
A special closet in the hall
To hold my magic brooms.

Enchanted woods around my home
Would shimmer in the night
With hippogriffs and unicorns
And phoenixes in flight.
Oh, what lovely time I'd have,
If wishes could come true,
And I was just a sorcerer,
Who knows what I could do?

J A Brown

The Wedding Guests

The ivory loveliness cossets you, so many things you meant to do,
You haven't even found the loo, and the wedding guests are piling through.
Old Uncle Cyril slyly winks and dashes off to grab a drink,
And as he lets Aunt Susan sink, you stretch one snow-white hand to link
Within your childhood's favourite arm, and also raise a lily palm
To greet a schoolfriend, calm a niece, and spread a magic bridal charm
Throughout the quickly filling hall. There's barely time to greet them all,
To take a photo, steal a small, quick wifely kiss before the call for dinner.

Your sister Jess becomes estranged from half her dress.
Cyril's gazing at her breasts. You shimmer up and just suggest
She'd perhaps want to readjust the lacework dangling from her bust
Before you have to turn and must, once more, be focal, fawned and fussed.
Your father now begins to talk about the time you learned to walk,
A colleague shares an office thought, an old flame becomes overwrought
And people that you barely know remember where you used to go,
And how you'd hold your head just so and how you'd let your anger show.

Perfectly the shining host, you play with food and leaving most,
Half-hear your husband's gentle boasts, and see them standing for the toasts,
And if it's true that all that live are just perceptions and remembrances
Then surrounded by your life's cast, this, becomes the point in time that is

The most alive you'll ever be. The consciousness you have can see
Its reflection in the memories of these your guests, your history,
So as you gaze around you may just need to wipe a tear away,
Before they raise a glass to say they love you too, on this, your wedding day.

Andrew George

THE MUSIC FESTIVAL, ROTHBURY 2002
THE TEN-YEAR-OLD HARPIST

So young, we saw her on one summer's day,
Light-hearted, has she come straight from the beach, you say?
Plastic shoes, scratched knees and skimpy cotton top.
Clear eyes and skin. Her hair a shining mop.
On her face there is no sign of stress.
Her fingers on the strings a light caress
Her child-sized harp it seems her dearest friend
Hours spent in its lone company; and to what end?
We listeners hear the rich reward of her endeavour
And gives the visitors such unexpected pleasure.

M P Stephenson

WINTERS IN BORROWDALE

Winters in Borrowdale
I remember still
Days when the snows lay deep
On each shining hill.

Days when we walked, we two,
Over Skiddaw's snow
Glittery - bright with frost
In the long ago.

Glistening frosty days
Clear and crisp and cold,
Evenings of suns that set
In a blaze of gold.

Nights when the pure white stars
In the jet-black sky
Shone on the path we trod,
My love and I.

Brightly the winter's moon
Round and silver - pale
Shone as we wandered home
Through the still, white dale.

Home to a curtained room
And a warm bright fire,
Everything, there, was ours
That we could desire.

Emma Kay

Rhyme For Our Time

I put my mind in, and on Him -
My Rock, on the 'rim',
And quietly look onward
With Grace t'go forward
Towards the Son -
The lovely One
At God's right hand -
All that He's planned
Shall stand, in His way
and we shall pray
for peace in our heart
as we make, yet another start!

Anon

The Road Safety Conscious Dog

(What this describes, I actually witnessed!)

I saw a dog today
Trotting along alone,
He didn't seem concerned at all,
Quite happy on his own:
He came up to a crossing
Looked coolly left and right
And sat down on the pavement
Because of a red light;
He waited with a patience,
In humans seldom seen
Sedately waiting for the light
To turn again to green;
And as it did the dog got up
All tail and legs and feet,
Looked left and right a second time
And walked across the street!

Nicholas Winn

The Silent Tramp

Danny sits in silence
    On a little seat outside the door
Dressed in tattered, ragged clothing
    Looking pensive and forlorn
Dark curly hair peeping from
    His silver-grey felt hat
Bright red waistcoat, sky blue shirt
    With dazzling yellow cravat
A faded, weatherbeaten old jacket
    Sporting grease spots on the sleeves
With shabby navy cord trousers
    Worn threadbare at the knees
Danny's dejected, he's got no prospects
    His rugged hands are black as soot
If only he had shoes to wear
    He wouldn't go barefoot
This man's greatest wish would be
    To whistle, shout and sing
But the odds are stacked against him
    He cannot do a thing
A poor stone tramp must be content
    To sit patiently and wait
For a brand new coat of paint to transform him
    And maybe change his fate.

Angela Moore

Beware Of Wave-Watching

If there is a storm in the offing,
We had better stay off the seafront.
Wave-watchers are risking
The sweeping and whisking
Motions of the channel bearing a gale's brunt.

Coastguards stopped their search at St Leonards
For a woman swept to sea while walking
With her husband on the promenade.
Never was a ramble more ill-starred!
For days after, locals were talking.

'She was last seen trying to swim back
To shore. People waded in to grab
Her arm.' Then fierce undertows
Stole her away, in a tempest's throes.
Her widower faces hostile blab.

Gillian Fisher

The Healer

Oh how you love your precious pain
Not professed, and unwanted yet needed again
In your rush to be free and your need to be right
You stand in the darkness away from the light
Your soul's latest journey you choose not to take
You've paid with your pain - it must be a mistake
But how can you know if you choose not to feel
You stand in the skin of the one who can heal.

Annmarie

Transience

I look at you but you're a stranger now
you avoid my eyes but I can feel your scorn.
Our love was as transient as the snow
which lies unspoilt in the suburban dawn,
before commuters turn it all to slush
and then the warmth of the day melts it all.
Our love was as transient as the lush
trees which so grace New England in the fall,
but then harsh winds scatter the leaves away,
the branches left with skeletal fingers
and like all things the fallen leaves decay.
But in my memory our love lingers
when an hour without you I could not bear,
now I close my eyes wishing you weren't there.

Guy Fletcher

Fashion Killer

'The hemline's rather short,' he said,
'The sleeves are far too long.
You must have been to Oxfam
And got it for a song.'

'You clearly need your glasses,'
She told him with a frown.
'You bought it for your mistress
The other side of town.'

'I love the scarlet rose motif,
The pattern edged in black.
See how well it mingles
With the bloodstains on the back?'

Peter Butler

A Gambling Man

Being a gambler all my life,
Has brought me nothing but strife.
My savings and more I gambled away,
I didn't exercise integrity in any way.

How can I face my family and friends
Knowing their way of life on me depends?
I lost the money they entrusted to me,
Even though I promised to invest wisely.

I won't always be able to hide,
The only way out is suicide!
A difficult decision I had to make,
Harder still is the action to take.

Silently I mouthed, 'I love you, goodbye,'
Jumped into the deep murky lake to die.
Leaving my beautiful daughter,
To stand staring into the water!

Rosemary Davies

HALF A SIN

Oft
tempted to just half a sin;
if half a fear
ne'er pressed to intervene or override,
I would see
behind desire's half open gate
and view the other half of sin
upon the other side.

I feel to taste of half a sin
when temptation's sap doth steam and rise,
and wonder,
dare I venture forth
into disappointment
or
surprise!

Diana Mudd

There Will Always Be Me

It's not to be big or especially bright
It's not to impress someone of great height
It's just to work hard and give of your best
It's just about caring for all the rest
Who get left behind because they feel small
For they are the most important of all
It's all about knowing your neighbour's needs
And planting the future with loving seeds
It's about being quiet and never unkind
It's about being hurt with forgiveness in mind
It's about give and take that's sometimes one-sided
It's about keeping secrets with trust confided
It's about being thankful for all that we share
It's all about knowing there's somebody there
It's all about saying it's not 'I' but 'we'
It's all just to tell you, there will always be me.

Janet Steele

THE YEAR 2003

Now it is 2003
I wonder how it's going to be,
As it passes on its way,
We must take it day by day.
We think of good times we have had,
When the sun has shone all day
And everything has gone our way,
We hope the time will come again,
When the sun will shine instead of rain,
And as winter turns to spring,
The birds will all begin to sing.

B Mason

BITTER HARVEST

Old wounds are deep. Night's spectres wax and wane
then wax once more before my sleepless eyes.
Its shades once thrust from memory, rise again;
night's dungeon walls resound with fevered cries;
with baleful whisperings and fierce demands . . .
I watch and wait and listen in the dark.
The clock stirs at last. Its reluctant hands
now shiver, sweep and falter to the mark.
Another instant dies as it began;
bearing to the end its bitter load.
Yet pain is not so brief. Each moment's span
but reaps again what each before has sowed;
the fruits of anguish in a tortured mind
that sees no peace ahead, no joy behind.

Steve J Waterfield

THERE'S LITTER ON OUR PAVEMENTS

There's litter on our pavements
On nearly every street

Have parents stopped teaching their children
That it's better to be neat?

Crisp packets, cans, sweet wrappers
Fish and chip papers too,

Pot Noodle containers, leftovers
Can make a huge rubbish stew.

Have people all stopped caring,
Is laziness the rule?

To drop one's litter anywhere
Is it now what they call 'real cool'?

Are litter bins just decoration?
Are we too tired to walk an odd yard

To place our litter safely away
Is it really so very hard?

When young, the streets were much cleaner.
The change is very great.

As children, we wouldn't dare make such mess
Else our parents would really create!

Other nations don't have the same problem
We've noticed when travelling abroad.

The streets are kept very clean
In each country that we've toured.

It used to be dogs fouling pavements
But that now seems under control,

So please let us pick up our litter
And make it our very next goal.

E Marcia Higgins

AN EMOTIONAL FINDING

(For Justine and John)

Lost an emotion - they're carried on a hospital wing,
Such a perfect tainted memory of a view of her and him,
A memory that can help remember all there is to know,
How purely fragile things are, how the present can simply go.
Fragile yes, but such a strength unseen,
And at your expense perhaps, we know what it is to mean.

Elizabeth Austin

AUTUMN LEAVERS

They soar from trees like starling flocks,
They scurry down the lane like mice,
When wet they're sly as kelp-strewn rocks,
When dry the crisp brown skin on rice.

In skittish whirls they rage through town,
As poltergeists mischief-obsessed,
They carpet lawns in red and brown
And swarm like plagues of stinging pests.

Recalcitrants firmly refuse
To join the sweeper's tidy heap;
They leap his broom, hide his shoes,
And scatter like unruly sheep.

Then one still day quite suddenly
They're turned to ash: a fate suffered
By withered mortals too, equally
Numerous and unremembered.

Alan W Ruffles

Story Of Love

You are the era of deep emotion
You are the mind of eternal devotion
You are the vision that delights the eye
You are the dawn in Aurora's sky
You are the nectar of the wine of love
You are the zephyr in the wings of a dove
You are the dream that really came true
You are the one and only you
You danced into my heart with the waltz of love
You kissed as an angel from Heaven above
You spoke to me gentle like whispering trees
I lay in your arms on the waves of the seas
You are the longing that sated my soul
You are the riches in life to unfold
You are the story of love that is told
Over and over and never grows old.

Agnes Lawson

The Fireman

I moved the coal that made the heat
That made the steam that drove the beat
That tap-danced down the silver rail
And raced the moon and vapour trail.
In black and white life's story told
By angry young men of the sixties mould
That sang the songs that moved the feet
And wrote the words the angel creaks.
When coal was king and steam the key
And dry mouths washed by cold stewed tea
In footplate days I moved the coal
To the people's sound of 'rock 'n' roll'.

John Grocutt

Bloody Games

In the underground terrain
someone's calling out a name,
someone shuffles, someone deals,
one man falls and someone kneels.
Is this cricket, is it poker?
Who's the ace and who's the joker?
Sexed-up paper in the bin
someone out there's suffering.
Democratic bullets flying
someone's grinning, someone's dying.
You make me sick, you bunch of fools,
is this fair play and where's the rules?

Jackie Davey

Senior Moments

You need a kick-start in the morning
Metaphorically speaking old son,
Your body is trying to tell you
It's too blinking knackered for fun.

Still ogling those girls in short dresses
Pretending you still know what's what
Then falling asleep on park benches
Bemused by newfangled G-spot.

When using your bus pass for travel
On day trips to places unknown
A senior moment then bingo -
You ask for erogenous zone.

It's time for some genteel persuasion
A little tea dancing maybe,
Or NHS lap dancing classes
Where anything goes and it's free.

Doreen Lovey

One For The Boys

(For Tamar)

Now all you boys
Who swagger and pose
You hurt my girl
I'll break your nose

You make her cry
You'll be in trouble
You give her gyp
I'll give you double

You mess with her
I'm at your door
You make her cry
I'll break your jaw

You give her grief
I'll give you flack
You break her heart
I'll break your back

You tell her lies
I'm on your case
You smash her dreams
I'll smash your face

I'll cut your heart
From out your chest
If you don't treat
My girl the best

Can I do that?
Yes I can
When I'm not Mum
I'm Jackie Chan

And if you think
This is a game
I've got your number
And your name

So boys, take note
Of what I said
You hurt my girl
Then you'll be dead.

Jacqui Shapiro

A Free View Of Nature

You've got to find a good seat
somewhere you can sit down and think;
somewhere with a wide window view where
you can sit to watch nature making stew.

If it rains think of the ingredients stirring
away in the highest storms. And don't worry
if it hurts you, it's just a kettle storm.

The sandstorm can be worst dear, because
it's not where you are. It's just a part of
porridge that you had before the storm.

When you see the sunlight forming, streaking
across the sky, you can share this golden
habit, of watching it with a smile.

Food is like your nature taking it in like
fast food. You like the taste of most everything
like the man smiling from the moon.

The world's mountains find it hard to see you
where you're sitting down at your window view.
You can imagine the snowbound peaks and
the silver water standing still.

The nuts still grow in the country and blackberry
as well, but you don't go out to find them
you're into market tin.

You get a free view of nature, and you get
the light and the dark; the light is full of
freckles and reminds you of a park.

Your children are all around you, ingredients
of your mind, toothpaste-white the willows bending
worlds away out of sight.

You don't shave like the summer, your face is
fresh and smooth, and winter keeps on turning, when
you buy new shoes.

David Rosser

EASTER 2003

The soldier scanned the desert waste
with practiced wary eye.
He watched an allied jet soar
into a darkening sky.
'If a bullet doesn't get me,
or a missile strike me dead,
I might be home for Easter,'
the valiant soldier said.

The pilot sent on a mission
had orders clear and concise.
To destroy a specific target
well, no one said war was nice!
'Barring accidents or capture,
if I can keep a cool head,
I might be home for Easter,'
the brave young pilot said.

A mother watched a TV screen,
her eyes were veiled in tears.
A pretty girl sobbed and mourned
for her lonely future years.
'Why my son? Why my love?
Why not someone else instead?'
'He won't be home for Easter now,'
a grieving father said.

They gave their lives for others
as the Son of God had done.
Following the way of truth and right,
not for glory or for fun.
So that each and everyone of us,
however we worship or pray,
will, with faith, find peace once more,
as we celebrate Easter day.

Sonja F Mills

My Rhyming Time

While time rides my declining life
I find my mind writhes in strife.
I whine, I cry, ninety-nine times:
Why, why die?

Then friends said,
'Dread of every threat
that tends to end in death offends
'n trends that send
messages questioning Heaven and Hell
never mend.'

I smiled my benign smile.
We breathed to feel the sweet freedom of peace

And had a cup-a-tea – camomile
if you please!

R J Westwell

YOUR NEW HOME

May this your humble dwelling place
See fit for all adventures new
And may joy be ever present here
For all those who flow close to you.
May gentleness and love surround you
Ever as you journey on
And may a place true peace can find you
Be here . . . in your new home.

Blanche Helena Hall

I'm Me

If I was black, would I be different?
Would I?
But I'm me, I'm me, still me.
Who said that I'm different?
Did you say it?
But I'm me, still me.
Who made me, me?
Did you make me?
Who made me?
God made me,
Did He?
Did He make me differently,
Did He?
Why did He?
Do you know why?
Are you saying you know
Don't you know?
But why am I different?
Am I?
But I'm me, still me.

Ann Murphy

CELEBRATE!

We celebrate three hundred years
Since Wesley saw the light -
Susannah's son, whose name was John,
He preached with all his might;
He went among the common folk
The gospel for to tell,
He rode a horse and preached outside -
He did it very well.

A Holy Ghost conviction fell
On sinners great and small,
Brought many to repentance
Who upon the Lord did call,
So Heaven's gates are open wide
The kingdom is expanding
And much to Father's great delight
The pit of Hell's disbanding.

The 'brand plucked from the burning'
Was to lift our spirits higher,
The heart that once was strangely warmed
Now set the world on fire.
The Methodists were born in song
To sing our Saviour's praise –
'Rejoice, again I say rejoice'
Through all your length of days.

Winnie Pat Lee

History Time

Twinkle, twinkle little star,
I often wonder how you are?

The Britons went up the Thames
To fetch a pail of water,
Then came down wearing a frown,
People were dying ever after.

London's burning,
London's burning,
Stomach's churning,
Stomach's churning,
Liar, liars, are the friars.
Children mourning,
Rich folk scorning.

First came disease and slavery,
Then came a new century.

Bullets rain, go away,
Come again no other day,
There are too few men here left to play.

All the Queen's women and all the Queen's men,
Had to put Britain together again.

Many days I often sigh . . .
History keeps repeating why?

Twinkle, twinkle little star,
I often wonder how you are?

Elizabeth Haruna

CATCH A DREAM

Stretch out your fingers and catch a dream,
The sway of the flowers, the sound of a stream.
The earth's smell of perfume after the rain,
The birds in the hedgerows, sweet songs their refrain.

Silver edge clouds in a deep purple sky,
Touching the moonlight as stars glide by.
The swish of the ocean, the sound of the sea,
The water like silk, sparkling and free.

The blackness of night, silent and still,
The peace of the heavens, beyond the hill.
No crying of seagulls, no sound in the air,
All nature sleeping, free from care.

The waves gently rolling as they ebb and flow,
The sea calls in whispers, softly and low.
Dawn slowing rising, a dim early light,
The owl hoots goodbye to a cool summer night.

Whispering wind, rustling trees,
Perfumed flowers, pounding seas.
The moon and the stars, the earth and the sun,
The wonderful things the Lord hath done.

Susie Field

Three Generations

When my mum was fifty, she thought that she was old,
She frowned at all the silver hairs scattered amongst the gold,
She tried her best to keep her youth and somehow envied me,
To have a daughter grown up, how ever could that be,
She argued and she worried, and told me once or twice,
When you get to my age dear, it won't be very nice.
When I got to fifty, nothing much did change,
I felt that I was still quite young, it didn't seem so strange.
My daughter now is fifty and has children of her own,
Their teenage ways refresh my years, I never seem alone.
My dress is still quite modern, my grandkids tell me so,
How I keep so fit and well, no one will ever know.
My secret is to laugh at life, there is so much to gain,
I won a cup as glamorous gran, and felt fifty once again.

Vera Parsonage

A Magic Night

There in the breeze
Leaves scatter in silence
Surveyed by the shining stars
Which capture your silhouette
Time is too soon

For we notice no passing
Of the pointless hours
We reside outside reality
Inside the bubble
Of youthful vitality.

Across the bay
Magic lights twinkle
Two hearts in harmony beat
And the ocean's task is simply to be
Generous with its wine-coloured spray.

Again we lay
Amid the haze of paradise
Beside the lake of Eternity
Until reality returns
With the light of a newborn day.

C O Burnell

TRAGEDY

The moon shone bright on that night
The tragedy did occur
As the train raced along
Jangling on its spur.

The fire fed 'til it turned red
The train sped along
And all was quiet
As the engine sang its song.

The wind swept down, the waters roared
Crashing near on high
As the bridge keeled over
With a mighty sigh.

The train bore down as all around
Lying and twisted there
The bridge so proud to become a shroud
For the passengers in despair.

The train plunged down without a sound
To sink beneath the waves
As for the passengers
The Forth became their graves.

J Lanigan

PERCEPTION OF LIFE

Lovely weeping willows that grace the river bank
Curtsey low with taste, relish and style.
They are aware of insight, acuteness, wisdom and vision,
A beautiful reflection
That looks back with a smile.

A sparrow hawk in swift flight and complete awareness
Speeds low along hedgerows,
While the kestrel hovers high with great observation,
Scanning the yellow fields, watching for his quarry
Among the corn and harvest home.

Along the river the kingfisher sits on an overhanging branch
Watching down the water course.
A brilliant flash of greenish-blue - a fish is caught.
Back on the branch, he eats with relish, showing little care or remorse.

Across the river naked to the sun,
A halo of purple, crimson and pink
Spreads its fragrance of heather
To bees, eager for nectar to drink,
And making honey, in the best of weather.

Along the highway and byway, one looks around,
Daisies and poppies begin to show, struggling between long coarse grass.
It becomes suddenly very quiet,
A feeling of walking on sacred ground.
One wonders perhaps he that one never sees
Has had a hand in this miracle, as well as the bees.

And when the sun tiptoes beyond the rim of light,
Honeysuckle floods the air with beautiful perfume and scent.
And when the stars open tired eyes and increase their sight,
They see the wonder of love; the miracle of life,
And gaze in sheer wonderment.

E S Peaford

DADDY'S LITTLE GIRL

I've always been Daddy's little girl,
But now I'm feeling lost.
I see you moving far away
To somewhere in the past.

More often now you seem confused,
I don't know what to do.
Is this Mother Nature's way
Of taking me from you?

We sit and talk, or try to,
About things that happened today.
Then suddenly you forget who I am,
Returning to yesterday.

You cared for me when I was young,
I will care for you now that you're old.
The decision I am forced to make
May anger you I'm told.

That's the chance I have to take
For you are my beloved father.
I want to keep you near forever,
Never leaving your loving daughter.

Our lifetime memories are happy ones,
I try hard not to be sad.
I will always be your little girl.
You will always be my dad.

Polly Davies

WANTED! REINCARNATION

'A holy, secret order held your past,'
A friendly woman told me once quite fast;
And lent me notebooks, arming me for strife
With wise quotations gathered through her life.

'What order did she mean by hinting so?'
I ask - the puzzle seems to grow and grow.
If we remembered past lives without doubt,
Such questions needn't promptly be ruled out.

One life provides us ample to forget,
As we all find as years go by; and yet
To know our evolution till this time
Would make our present less without a rhyme.

In fact, three-score-and-ten alone are not
Enough to get to know ourselves a lot.
We must insist on some before as well
As after, for a worthwhile tale to tell.

Allan Bula

All Work Without Rest Undoubtedly Kills

All work without rest undoubtedly kills,
Just pause for a moment, lest you should tire,
What always happens, the telephone shrills.

Mixing up concrete for window ledge sills,
Covered in dust and knee-deep in mire,
All work without rest undoubtedly kills.

Needing fresh clothing, the bath nearly fills,
Appointment is pressing, urgent and dire.
What always happens, the telephone shrills.

Worries enough, economies on bills,
Just settling down to accounts by the fire,
All work without rest undoubtedly kills.

Feet up and gazing at faraway hills,
Dreaming and listening to heavenly choir,
What always happens, the telephone shrills.

Man born to labour in ungodly mills,
To peace and tranquillity he must aspire,
All work without rest undoubtedly kills,
What always happens, the telephone shrills.

Tony Wade

PERPLEXED

'Why won't these carrier bags open?'
I curse through gritted teeth,
Under fire from lashing tongues and moans
It happens every week.

Clutching onto a friend's wedding list
Testing push button screens
Everyone else knows what to do
Apart from me it seems.

Confused by automatic flushes
Trolleys with coins and chains
Video timers, e-mailing and
Ticket machines for trains.

Perplexed, I gold my friend this problem,
Dejected, feeling lack of self worth.
Tossing her red hair she laughed and said,
'You must be a genius by birth.'

C Silvester

THE REVOLUTION

On return we found that the situation was retrievable because retroactive revolutionaries are retrainable with a small retainer and much retsina, although with regret, the reticent and the retaliatory will be retired.

I am relieved to know that the reverence of revolution that was relevant in Revelania is re-valued so that revulsion of revolutionaries mean reveille and revolvers are reviled. The revisionists can now revenge revolutionaries and revise the revolt that happened in our reverential land.

Even so, after the rise it is risqué to rival the risen and ringleaders can expect to RIP. For the righteous the road has become rocky, but respect will be rewarded with rank.

As Rousseau might once have reminisced, 'they now revel in the roughage from our rectum and rebuild with our rejected regalia as we have successfully revolted.'

Adam Cohen

DRIVEN

Our love is like traffic lights
another woman around
and you turn green,
I turn red, then yellow
and prepare to move off
swiftly.

Our love is like a car
driving us on,
sometimes breaking down.
Last year's model fits
in the glove compartment
of memory.

Our love is like the road,
sometimes taking us down
routes we know intimately;
at others, unexpected turns
take us to new vistas.

Charles Hurst

SLUG

Well who could love a slug,
Such a slimy 'bug'
He eats up your flowers
After a shower
What's there to like about that?

Move on to the snail
With her silvery trail
Delicate shell,
She casts a spell
So what if she nibbles my lettuce.

Fred's there in his web
An orb spider under the window
Web of perfection
And patterned back
Would make Miss Muffet proud!

And after I've marvelled at
All of this nature
The slugs and snails have had a convention
And eaten my garden - howzat!

E Osmond

EQUAL AGAIN

In the beginning was woman and man.
The beginning of the almighty plan.
On the average, man was larger and somewhat stronger.
To even things up, women on average lived a little longer.
From the time of stone-age man to men in bowlers who worked in the city,
Man went to work, woman stayed at home, having babies and looking pretty.

All seemed fair, we jogged merrily along,
But something was amiss, something drastically wrong.
An error in the world had been made, in the east, west, north and the south.
Women had gained an advantage, they had a tongue to wag in their mouth.

Even the strongest man with a will of iron would begin to sag
After hours and hours of that continuous nag.
No man could cope with that perpetual wag.
An answer had to be found, it was a difficult problem,
Was there any way to lick it?

England found the answer, they invented a game,
A game called, namely, cricket!

Deep square-leg, mid-wicket, first slip, silly point.
These strange terms put a woman's mouth and brain out of joint.
All women love to argue, but what they hate is to look and sound like fools.
Even the 'know-alls' keep quiet, baffled by cricket's queer names and rules.

Man was free again, free to shout, 'I'm off to cricket, would you like to go?'
Safe in the knowledge the answer would be a loud and resounding 'No!'

The sexes were equal again, man in the ladder of life
Had been allowed to climb an extra rung.
England found the answer, cricket.
The one thing to silence even a woman's tongue.

David Sim

Projectile Vomiting As A Means Of Social Dominance

I'm writing a serious scientific paper for a psychological journal.
There isn't time to tell you the details so I'll just give you the kernel.
It's about our little ginger cat, how in our household he
achieved prominence.
I will call it 'Projectile vomiting as a means of social dominance.'

I need to explain that Ginger is very weak and small.
You'd never think he'd come out top of the heap at all.
But his infallible weapon for intimidating each member of our house is
A stomach full of cat food and explosive reverse peristalsis.

We've got a large and bouncy dog, an innocent sort of chap.
He has a bed in the kitchen in which he takes a nap.
Now Ginger goes and sleeps in it, and what causes the dog to grieve,
Is that the cat pukes up in it before he takes his leave.

We've got a second cat, a tabby Tom, a hulking bruiser is he.
He's got a food bowl in the conservatory in which we put his tea.
But while old Tom's back is turned, before he's had a chance to sup it,
Ginger sneaks up, has a quick sneer, and quietly throws up in it.

My son came home from college with a holdall full of books,
He dumped it in the kitchen, he's less smart than he looks.
Ginger quickly found it, his aim was straight and true,
He got the holdall and the books, and the zip and handle too.

So, if you come to our house, I advise you to take care.
If you go into the front room and sit in Ginger's chair
He'll meekly come and sit at your feet, you'll think
'What a nice little chap!'
So fluffy and sweet, small and neat.
Don't let him sit on your lap!

B W Ford

ETHEL'S PARTY

90, 90! What a day!
Not feeling *that* old I must say.
With good friends, still having fun,
I'd like to get to 91.
There's still a lot I'd like to do,
Lord, could I please see 92?
93. Now that's a good score,
But better still is 94.
If life's still good to be alive,
I wouldn't mind reaching 95.
If it's OK, Lord, could You fix
A use for me at 96?
At 97, with hopes of Heaven,
Or 98, near the pearly gate,
Such memories to pass the time
Till I get to 99.
And *if* I reach my century
I'll need to fix another tea!

Margaret Lawley

Crab Capers

He was a crab among the rocks, feeling rather jolly,
Nearby was a lobster, the cause of all this folly.
'Have I seen you here before?' said the crab, to get acquainted,
Lobster then got quite a fright, in fact she almost fainted.

'Come and have a little walk among the seaweed here,'
'No thanks,' said lobster, 'your sideways walk seems a little queer.'
But the crab was not dismayed, he stood so very proudly,
He took a step, just to one side, his pincers snapping loudly.

Other shellfish all around sat and watched in wonder,
Crab by now was having doubts, perhaps he'd made a blunder.
Undeterred he tried again, perhaps Lobster would not wait,
He sidled near her, trailing sand, with a most ungainly gait.

To a party then they went, in fact they had a rave,
The sea was calm, they came ashore on a little wave.
Crab was walking straight and true, 'What's wrong?' the lobster hissed.
'Please be quiet,' he whispered back, 'I think I'm slightly p****d.'

Alister H Thomson

ALIEN INVASION

It started off with one or two,
Until they invaded in force:
Dangerous alien machines,
Infiltrating without remorse.

Choosing those older and infirm,
They need humans to move around,
Who become reliant on them,
Together making little sound.

The humans are expressionless,
Consumed by the alien race.
From each corner of our pavements,
They move at a determined pace.

They disappear when it is dark.
It seems that they dislike the night.
then they emerge during the day,
With their hosts in hours of daylight.

Might the aliens be friendly,
Travelling to our world in peace,
In the guise of motor scooters,
To give housebound humans release?

What the future holds is unclear,
But it seems they are here to stay.
Will I be a scooter driver,
Another host on the pathway?

I hope so, if I could not walk
And a struggle just to get out:
Then I would thank the aliens,
For getting me out and about.

Janet N Hewitt

STATIONARY

The air is still; the oaks share their secrets.
A small breeze squeezes through gaps in the fence.
One yellow leaf scuffles off the platform,
falling out of the wind, onto the rail.
A train hurries through - the air goes crazy -
leaves are thrown up, buffeting, billowing,
zooming along beside, behind the train.
Slowly, they settle. A single leaf stirs.

Gill Smith

LAMENTATION

Wind is sighing,
The earth is dying.

Gone lush greens
And summer's blues,
Replaced by a cloak
Of autumnal hues.
Grey sky sheds a tear,
Shards of icy rain;
The leaves are falling
Down each country lane.

Nature withers, dies
Beneath glowering skies.

Geraldine Laker

AUTUMN

The sun goes down in the west
On mellow fruitfulness of autumn.
Gold, rusty leaves of a copper beech -
Myriad colours of reds and browns.
The evening chorus of song
Like a church choir.
The wild geese emigrating to warmer climates.
Season of richness and ripeness,
Autumn is of the heart.

I T Hoggan

October Night

This cool October night
is filled with sounds
in which my ears and eyes delight
chattering crickets join whistling frogs
in a song whose rhythm defies meaning.

Across the way a dog now bays
at the rising moon,
a cat slinks by, her watchful eye
fixed upon her mortal enemy.

The breeze now runs her fingers
through the trees
whose languid leaves shiver
and dance to an unsung tune.

How different colours are at night
no pungent shadows or hues too bright
but all submerged in a sombre glow
of greys and darker pigments.

But now that too begins to change
as from behind a sheltering cloud,
the moon emerges and bathed below,
the landscape glows in bluish silvery light.

P L Brassington

OCTOBER

Looking out the window
across the street,

Trees wave in the October breeze,
their leaves,
brown, golden and red,
soon will fall
tumbling down to the dewy ground.

Autumn,
winter comes in your wake.
Season of earth's sleep.

Helen Marley